EASY DANCES FOR SOLO PIANO

86 Pieces for Early and Intermediate Players

Selected by

HAROLD WOLF

D1736466

DOVER PUBLICATIONS, INC.
Mineola, New York

Bibliographical Note

This Dover edition, first published in 2004, is a new compilation of music previously published in earlier Dover editions.

International Standard Book Number: 0-486-43800-7

Manufactured in the United States of America
Dover Publications, Inc., 31 East 2nd Street, Mineola, N.Y. 11501

CONTENTS

Zortzico*

(from *España,* op. 165, 1890)

Isaac Albéniz
(Spain, 1860–1909)

*An old Basque dance in quintuple time in which the rhythm is marked on a percussion instrument.

sf
p
sf
p

dolce
poco rit.
a tempo
pp
ff
mf

sf
p
pp
cresc.
f
sf
sotto voce
ff

From English Suite No. 2: Two Bourrées and Gigue

Johann Sebastian Bach
(Germany, 1685–1750)

Bourrée I.

Bourrée II.

Gique.
1.
2.

1.
2.
Fine.
Da Capo
dal Segno
(senza repetizione)
al Fine.

From English Suite No. 3: Sarabande and Two Gavottes

Johann Sebastian Bach

Sarabande.

Gavotte I.

Gavotte II.
(ou la Musette.)

From English Suite No. 6: Two Gavottes

Johann Sebastian Bach

Gavotte I.

Gavotte II.

From French Suite No. 2:
Courante

Johann Sebastian Bach

From Partita No. 1: Two Minuets and Gigue

Johann Sebastian Bach

Menuet II.
Gique.

Six Minuets

(WoO 10, 1795)

Ludwig van Beethoven
(Germany & Austria, 1770–1827)

No. 1.

No. 2.

No. 3.
sf
ff
sf
Trio.
p
sf
sf
f
1.
2.
1.
2.
sf
sf
sf
sf
Men. da capo.

No. 4.
Trio.
Men. da capo.

No. 5.

No. 6.

Six Ländler

(WoO 15, 1802)

Ludwig van Beethoven

Nº 1.

Nº 2.

No. 3.
sf
sf
No. 4.
No. 5.
sf
sf
sf
sf
sf
sf
sf
sf
sf

sf
sf
Nº 6.
CODA.

sf
sf
sf
sf
sf
sf
f

Three Waltzes

(Nos. 2, 3 and 11 from *Waltzes,* Op. 39, 1865)

Johannes Brahms
(Germany & Austria, 1833–1897)

2

3

1.
2.
11
fp
p
più legato
dim.
p dolce

"Minute" Waltz in D-flat Major

(Op. 64, No. 1, 1847)

Frédéric Chopin
(Poland & France, 1810–1849)

sostenuto

tr
f
p
Ped.

pp
f
Ped.

Waltz in A Minor

(Op. 34, No. 2, *c.* 1834)

Frédéric Chopin

Sostenuto.

pp
Ped.
tr

Sostenuto.
f
p
pp
tr

tr
pp
Ped.
poco riten.
a tempo
tr
tr

Mazurka in C Major

(Op. 7, No. 5, *c.* 1832)

Frédéric Chopin

Dal Segno senza Fine.

Mazurka in B-flat Major

(Op. 7, No. 1, *c.* 1830)

Frédéric Chopin

a tempo
poco rall.
sotto voce
pp
a tempo
rubato
poco rall.
cresc.
1.
2.
Ped.

Mazurka in F Major

(Op. 68, No. 3, *c.* 1832)

Frédéric Chopin

Poco più vivo.
p
riten.
Tempo I.
f
p
Ped.

Passepied

(from *Suite Bergamasque,* 1890/1905)

Claude Debussy
(France, 1862–1918)

più f
f
p
mf
dim.
p

sf
p
più p
cédez un peu
mf
a tempo
p
p
p

mp
sf
pp
mf
cresc.
sf
cresc.
f

pp
cédez - - - - - - a Tempo
pp
rit.
a tempo
ppp
ppp

pp
molto
dim.
I° tempo
p
f

dim.
f
p
più p
sempre p
sf
mf
dim.

p
più p
pp
rit.
a Tempo
pp
pp
ppp
ppp

Golliwogg's Cake-Walk

(from *Children's Corner,* 1906–8)

Claude Debussy

più p
più p
Un peu moins vite

pp
<pp>
Cédez
p avec une grande émotion
a Tempo
p
pp
Cédez
a Tempo
Cédez
a Tempo
mf
f
Cédez
a Tempo
Cédez

a Tempo
p
pp
f
ff
f
p
p
Retenu
dim.
più p
pp
pp
Toujours retenu
pp
1º Tempo
p
p
molto
f
sff

p cre - scen - do
f ff
p
p
p
f sff
p
p
f
f ff
p
p
p
f
ff
ff

Spanish Dance No. 2 (Orientale)

(from *12 Danzas Españolas, c.* 1888-90)

Enrique Granados
(Spain, 1867–1916)

pp
poco cresc.
pp
p dolce
dim.
rit.
pp
Lento assai.
p
f
dim.
p

rit. un poco
a tempo
p
dim.
una corda
f
rit. e dim.
p
Andante.
p
dolce

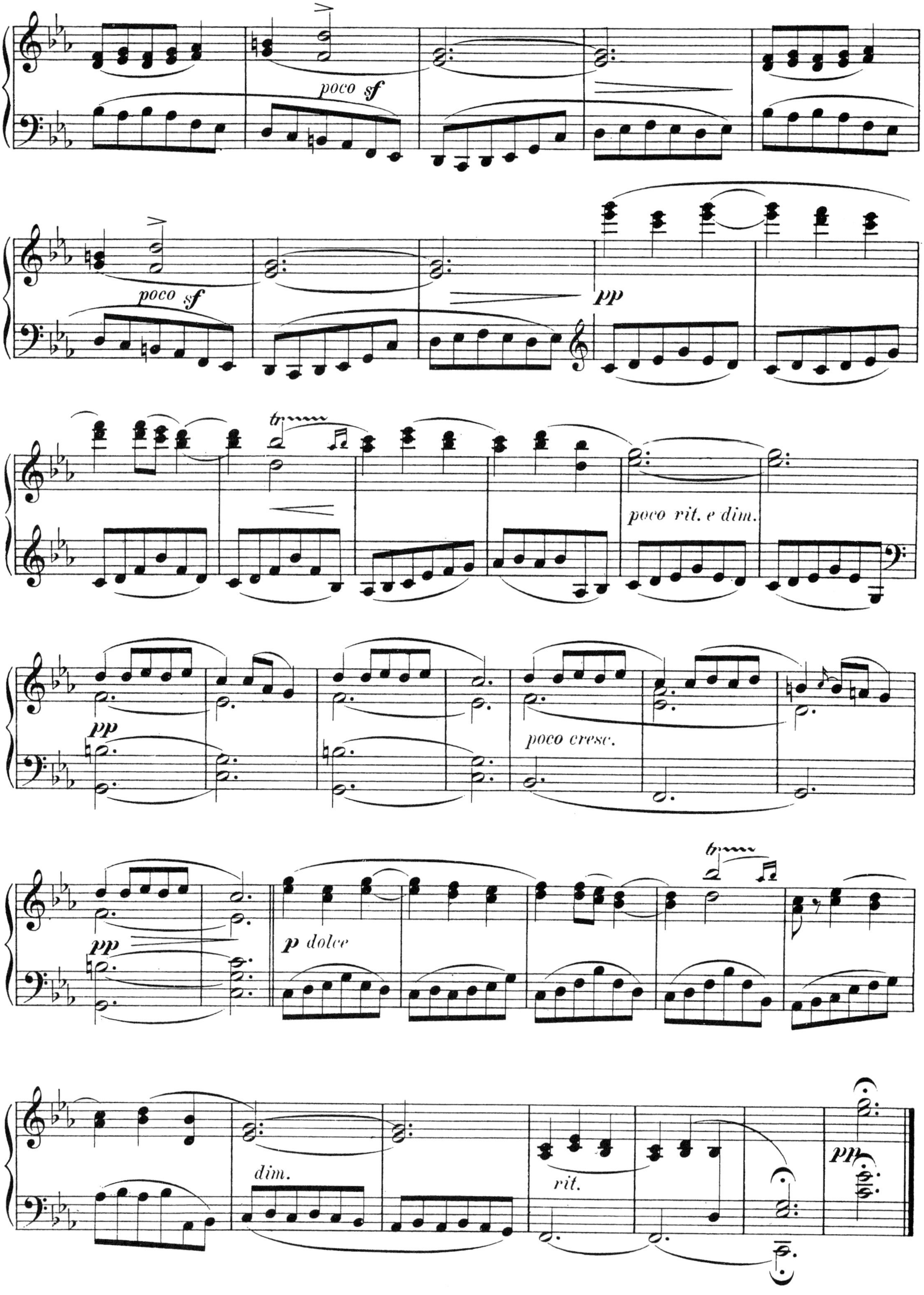
poco sf
poco sf
pp
tr
poco rit. e dim.
pp
poco cresc.
pp
p dolce
tr
dim.
rit.
pp

Spanish Dance No. 4 (Villanesca)

(from *12 Danzas Españolas, c.* 1888-90)

Enrique Granados

Andante espress.
a tempo

Andante espressivo.
a tempo
rit.
Cancion y estribillo.
Molto Andante.
poco cresc.
tr
rit.
cresc.
poco dim.
tr
rit.
a tempo

poco a poco cresc.
ff
8
12

Andante espressivo.
a tempo
12
8
12
Andante espress.
rit. molto e dim.
pp

Two Poetic Waltzes

(from *Valses Poéticos, c.* 1894)

Enrique Granados

Tempo de Valse noble
2.
rubato
rall.
a tempo
dim.
con molta fantasia
pp
rit.
vivo
pp
cresc.
rubato
8
Adagio
pp

rubato
rall.
a tempo
con molta fantasia
pp
rit.

Valse-Impromptu

(No. 1 from *Lyric Pieces,* Op. 47, 1886–8)

Edvard Grieg
(Norway, 1843–1907)

Allegro con moto.

m.s.
m.s.
Tempo I.
pp
f
sempre
f
pp
poco
tranquillo
tr
ritard.
a tempo
p
rubato
cresc.
rubato

fz
pp
stretto molto e cresc.
f
rit.
molto
molto più lento
cantabile
m.s.
m. s.
p
pp
Ped.
Tempo I.
pp
f
sempre
f
pp
poco

tr
tranquillo
ritard.
a tempo
p
rubato
cresc.
rubato
fz
pp
stretto molto e cresc.
f
rit.
molto
molto più
cantabile
lento
m. s.
p
m. s.
pp
ppp
Ped.

Halling (Norwegian Dance)

(No. 4 from *Lyric Pieces,* Op. 47, 1886–8)

Edvard Grieg

Leaping Dance

(No. 6 from *Lyric Pieces,* Op. 47, 1886–8)

Edvard Grieg

Ped.
p
pp
cresc.
molto
ff
dim.
ppp

Anitra's Dance

(No. 3 from *Peer Gynt Suite No. 1,* Op. 46, 1888)

Edvard Grieg

*) The trills without concluding notes.

tr
pp
f
f
p
fp
fp
fp
fp

tr
mf
pp
fp
cresc.
f
fz
dim.

a tempo
ritard.
p
mf
pp
f
tr
1.
2.

Minuet in G Major

(K. 1/1e, 1761)

Wolfgang Amadeus Mozart
(Austria, 1756–1791)

Menuetto da Capo al Fine.

Minuet in F Major

(K. 2, 1762)

Wolfgang Amadeus Mozart

Minuet in F Major

(K. 4, 1762)

Wolfgang Amadeus Mozart

Minuet in D Major

(K. 355/576b, *c.* 1787)

Wolfgang Amadeus Mozart

mancando
dolce
f
p
f
p
f
p
f
p

Allemande

(from *Premier livre de pieces de clavecin*, *c.* 1706)

Jean-Philippe Rameau
(France, 1683–1764)

1ª
2ª

Vénitienne

(from *Premier livre de pieces de clavecin*, c. 1706)

Jean-Philippe Rameau

Menuet

(from *Premier livre de pieces de clavecin*, c. 1706)

Jean-Philippe Rameau

Gymnopédie No. 1

(1888)

Erik Satie
(France, 1866–1925)

1ST GYMNOPAIDIKE [Spartan dance of naked youths and men]. Slow and sorrowful.

p

pp
pp
f
pp

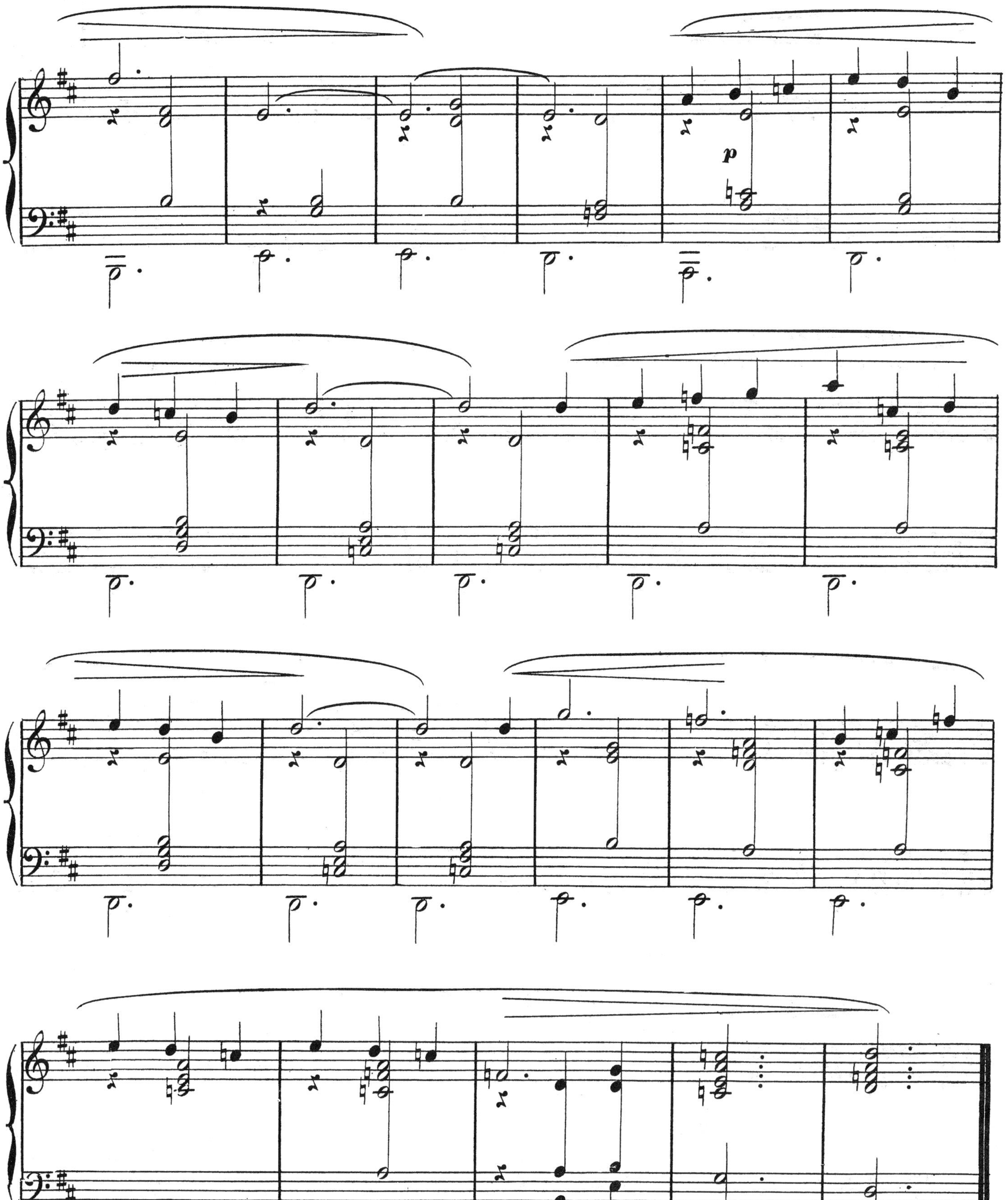
p

Gnossienne No. 1

(1890)

Erik Satie

GNOSSIENNE [Dance of ancient Knosos, Crete (?)] (1890). Slow. Very shiny. Ask.

With the tip of your thought. Postulate within yourself. Step by step. On the tongue.

17 Ländler

(D. 366, 1816–24)

Franz Schubert
(Austria, 1797–1828)

Nº 3.

Nº 4.

Nº 5.

Nº 6.

Nº 7.

№ 8.

№ 9.

№ 10.

Nº 11.
Nº 12.
p
pp
cresc.
Nº 13.
tr
mf
Nº 14.
(p)

1.
2.
№ 15.
fp
№ 16.
№ 17.
p
mf

8 Ecossaises

(D. 299, 1815)

Franz Schubert

Nº 1.

Nº 2.

Nº 1. D. C.

No. 3.

No. 4.

No. 3. D. C.

No. 5.

Nº 6.
p
ff
Nº 5. D. C.
Nº 7.
mf
3
Nº 8.
p
f
Nº 7. D. C.

Gigue

(Op. 32/2, 1838–9)

Robert Schumann
(Germany, 1810–1856)

Sehr schnell. ♩. = 116.

ritard.
Ped.

Ländler

(No. 15 from *Albumblätter,* Op. 124, 1854)

Robert Schumann

Waltz

(No. 7 from *Albumblätter,* Op. 124, 1854)

Robert Schumann

Impromptu à la Mazur

(Op. 2/3, 1886–9)

Alexander Scriabin
(Russia, 1872–1915)

On the Beautiful Blue Danube

(Op. 314, 1867)

Johann Strauss, Jr.
(Austria, 1825–1899)

Introduction.
Andantino.

Waltz.

2.
mf
1.
f
p
2.
Close.
dol.
Fine.
dol.
pp
p
mf
Dal Segno senza repetizione al Fine.
3.
p
p cresc.
f
1.
p
2.
p
p

1.
2.
Ending.
4.
Intrada.
Waltz.
1.
2.
1.
2.
Ending.

Intrada.
5.
Waltz.
1.
2.

1.
2.
ff
p
Coda.
p
cresc.
p
p
mf
f
p
f
f
tr
pp
p

f
p
Ped.

ff
Ped.
fz
fz
1
p
pp
din.
cresc.
f

Pizzicato-Polka

(written with Josef Strauss, 1870)

Johann Strauss, Jr.

ff
p molto stacc.
ff
p
D. C. al segno, poi Coda.
Coda.
Più Allegro.
ff

Danse Russe

(Op. 40/10, 1878)

Peter Ilyitch Tchaikovsky
(Russia, 1840–1893)

Andantino

f
sf
p
dim.
m.d.
ritard.
m. s.

Allegro molto vivace
f
sf
sf
sf
sf
sf

p poco a poco cresc.
ff

Mazurka

(No. 11 from *Album for the Young,* Op. 39, 1878)

Peter Ilyitch Tchaikovsky

sf
sf
p
mf
p
smorz.

Polka

(No. 10 from *Album for the Young,* Op. 39, 1878)

Peter Ilyitch Tchaikovsky